Clear-Light Living

Meditation
Volume 1

HÜMÜH Transcendental Buddhist

MATICINTIN
Wisdom Master

Dharmavidya Publishing
2009

Living Meditation

International Copyright © 2009 Maticintin
Printed in the United States of America
Dharmavidya Publishing

ISBN: 978-0-932927-27-9

Second Printing: 2009
First Printing: 2008

Scribe: Mary Daniels
Cover Design: Monika Mueller

DHARMAVIDYA PUBLISHING

P.O. Box 2700, Oroville, WA 98844 USA
or P.O. Box 701, Osoyoos, B.C. V0H 1V0 Canada
Phone/fax (250) 446-2022 / Phone Orders (800) 336-6015
E-mail:DharmavidyaPublishing@HUMUH.org

Table of Contents

Maticintin
Wisdom Master

Wisdom Master Maticintin is a vessel of the Mind Treasure Teachings, gifted her by the Transhistorical Consciousness, meaning she attained enlightenment in another lifetime. The Wisdom Master also has a Doctorate in Logic and Buddhism and is the Founder and Spiritual Leader of HÜMÜH: Transcendental Buddhism, Path to Enlightenment. The Wisdom Master currently teaches at a variety of HÜMÜH Meditation Centers in the United States, as well as at HÜMÜH Monastery and Skycliffe Retreat Centre in British Columbia. She also travels and teaches at other locations in the United States, Canada, and, occasionally, abroad.

Wisdom Master Maticintin is a noted author with many books to her credit, among them a fresh, poetic rendering and commentary on *The Heart Sutra*, and *The Golden Spiral: Handbook for Enlightenment*. Recognized as being a Buddhist for more than 30 years, she is also widely known as the Shaman Winged Wolf.

While keeping up with a year-round Teaching schedule, the Wisdom Master maintains periods of solitude in between working with her students and takes time to be in companion energy with a herd of 50 wild deer, a horse named Spirit, a donkey called Pepe, and a romping red-haired Pomeranian named Dorje.

She brought forth HÜMÜH as a new Buddhist sect in 1992 as an expression of the highest Teachings culled from all Buddhism to address the Western body/mind connection. One of the manifestations of her dedication as a Teacher is the Home-Study program she has developed that enables students to work with her at a distance, as well as through on-site retreats and classes. The spiritual path of HÜMÜH began in the United States and has rapidly expanded into Canada, while developing membership in a variety of other countries.

Living Meditation
Introductory Remarks

Living meditation is referred to and taught in this manner: *Be constantly aware of the light*, all the time. Because of this very fact that *everything is light*, if we have an *awareness* of all the light in our life, we have a *living meditation*. The sitting meditation that you participate in is to truly *revive* this part of yourself, to *attune* yourself to the light in its most *primordial* form....*Primordial form* means you're not focused on objects; instead, you're *focused mainly on the inner light*.

The more that you can *recognize* inner light, this inner light, then, *is what you see* everywhere around you. Your *sitting meditation is simply to focus on the inner light* and nothing else, and you allow the light to *enlarge*. Yes, images may pass through....they're 'scenes' *within the light*. You don't fixate on them, or become fascinated by them, because they're just scenes within the light, 'passing fancies,' so to speak. Not fantasies—*fancies*. It's a 'fancy' to see flashes of light, or contrasting images of light reflections. It's a fanciful feeling that goes on, not fantasy. In other words, it's taking bits and pieces of light and *ornamenting* your world with it.

By putting this flower here (on the table), I have ornamented the table, and because it's constantly throwing me a little gold light in my right eye (peripheral vision), I have a *little fancy* over there. Flowers contain a natural light. They have the inner light that they carry within themselves because they are living things. *Everything that's living contains a natural light.* The flowers are here, and they 'make fancy' with me. In my world, I have all this light, and you're here and I see your lights rise up and I see them diminish, so I see fanciful movements (not fantasy). When you recognize something, the light rises, and when you don't recognize something, the light diminishes, so quickly pull that light up again. It's *light-plays* constantly...*light-plays* all the time.

Living Meditation itself is something that you can *prove* to yourself in a very scientific way—how it exists in you, and how it can live out from you, as well. Here's the thing: *you are not your body.* You have to accept that premise first. You know your body dies, so *you* can't *be* your body. The very fact that your body dies means that's *not* you, because *you* are something that is *using* this body as a *vehicle.* You can feel that if you consider it.

8

Discovering the Energy Stream
& Energy Signatures

What I want you to do is close your eyes. When you close your eyes, you are going to see a light stream, or some kind of energy. There may be different colors, and depths, and whirlpools, and different things. Now, take your hand and pass it in front of your face. Close your eyes and make your hand pass in front of your face. Move your hand in front of your face, and then move it back away from your face. Notice the variations of what you see when you do that. If someone walked up to you while you had your eyes closed in that manner, you would get a completely different energy stream than the one you have with your own hand in front of your face.

The energy stream that you see when you close your eyes is affected by the movement of your energy and the movement of other energies around you. If you become accustomed to this stream of energy that you have with your eyes closed, then you'll understand the stream of energies that takes place with your eyes open.

If you close your eyes again for just one moment, right now, you'll see that there's like a little, mottled matrix inside, and the matrix looks like dots, rather than lines drawn this way and that way. Mostly, it looks like little dots of light and dark, light and dark. The dark also is light, incidentally, but darkness and light—that's a contrast. The darkness is really light that is *intense* and so it *appears* dark; but that's what gives you the contrast. What you see with your eyes closed is like an *energy signature* that gives your body life. That which gives your body life is actually that *divinity* you carry which motivates this body, brings this body to life.

So here you are—*divinity wearing a body*, and your *proof* of that is actually this *energy signature*, which, if you were dead, would not be there. Someone who is dead does not keep the energy signature inside of their body. It can't be viewed; so the very fact that you *can* view that energy signature means that you're alive. That *energy signature*—your *divinity* itself—is making that life movement inside of you. That's the energy signature, the *life movement*. That's your proof that you are alive, and that's your proof that you are divinity.

Do you ever wake up in the night? As you wake up in the night, notice the energy as it's being portrayed to you with your eyes closed. Then, see the energy in front of you and what it looks like, the designs that it's making. You'll find that in the middle of the night, the energy signature itself is just a stipple without any movement. This is because you woke up from your sleep, and as you woke up from sleep, there's nothing really moving. It just has a mottled, stippled look to it. When you wake up in the middle of the night, if it's really dark outside, then you can see that, yes, it's totally dark with your eyes closed, but at the same time, there is light on. The light that is turned on is the *light of consciousness*, the light of the *prajna*. This *prajna* light that exists with your eyes closed is the divinity, so it has the same power so that when you open your eyes, you can see matter. You're actually projecting the *prajna* of your closed eyes into the environment when you open your eyes. That's the *as above, so below* type-of-thing; *as within, so it is without.* This is what you need to be aware of—just to carry that around with you.

As you become accustomed to paying attention to this energy signature inside of yourself, you discover that you have this *inward light* that *takes different forms.* Maybe it will appear like a stream running through. Sometimes, with your eyes closed, you'll see the energy as a *stream*, rather than little dots. Maybe it will take actual *forms*, according to your state of consciousness at the time. It may take the form of a pyramid, or it may take various forms that you see in outer life. The very fact that it takes these forms is just conforming to your state of consciousness in that moment.

The Energy Signature
and Karma

The state of consciousness that you carry with you is reflected in your *outer* life. When you open your eyes, what you *see* around you is part of that state of consciousness. *It's the energy signature that you carry within you that is projected outward.* As you're thinking about what you're seeing, you're beginning to tell yourself different *definitions* of what you're seeing, and then you relate that to *feelings* that you have in relationship to this part of yourself that you <u>call</u> '*self.*' *That part of yourself that you call 'self' is really karma.* It's <u>not</u> your *Self*; it's <u>not</u> your *divinity*; it's <u>not</u> the same as the *energy signature*. The energy signature just 'takes shape' according to the *karma identity* that you carry. 'Karma' meaning everything that you have internalized as a feeling is now a part of your karma that you carry with you and influences the way you decide how you feel about things—your attitudes and opinions, and all that sort of thing. All these attitudes, all these opinions that you have a storehouse of—*that* has become your karma.

Your karma actually goes back *beyond birth*, because if you have several members of your family, several siblings, you'll notice that you are very different from each sibling. It's not just a matter of how you were raised. It's how you are a *composite of that karma* from birth. Yes, you do take on part of your mother and father, but you still have that composite of karma at birth that you came in with. That's why you're different from your siblings. So these attitudes and opinions are long-past.

Here you are carrying these attitudes and opinions from the distant past, and all the attitudes and opinions that you've accumulated from this lifetime, as well, and it taints your feelings as you open your eyes and look around the world. You have tainted feelings about this, that, and the other thing—*attitudes*; and these attitudes 'warp,' or distort, the *pure energy signature* into various forms. The energy signature—if you were to measure your brain waves on a chart, the chart would go up and down, and sideways, and all these different ways to give you a signal, a signature of yourself and how you're thinking. The energy signature is a purer form of such a mechanical interpretation. You can see what that is just by looking at it yourself. When you're very upset, and you look at that energy signature, that energy signature is doing all sorts of things. It might produce colors in the energy signature about the feelings that you have.

You can learn a lot about yourself through becoming aware of the energy signature that you carry. That energy signature—just because of what you see now—doesn't mean it can't change and become something else all the time, because it will. You change *constantly*. As you are learning something that is *outside* of your normal way of seeing life, you begin to change. This energy signature then produces more and more *refined imagery*; so therefore, when you open your eyes, what you see all around you is more and more refined. The refinement that you view *within*, then is projected *outward*.

The very fact that you have an energy stream means that *you're all light*. You are all light; *every particle of your being is light.*

Watching the
Energy Stream

Before you had a body, when you were part of the Void...before you had *experience* in a body, long, long ago,...before you had *any* experience in a body, you were a *pure light being*. A pure light being, in the Void *sense*, looked like this (*See* Illustration A)—not in a circle, necessarily; it could be just vast openness—that's what this is intended to imply.

Illustration A

Here you are—you are nothing but light. If you look at Illustration A, which shows a dark circle, you say, "That's not light." But it *is* light. It is real, *intense* light. Astronomers see things as they gaze up into the heavens—and the sky is 'the heavens.' In between planets, there are dark, dark, dark places that are far, far, far-away places. These far, far-away places are just *blackness*. That's how they are portrayed: as black holes, black space. *You are a part of that black space in your original form.* That black space is more than what we think of as 'space.' It is actually the Void itself. You are *That* in your *primal* body, which is *no body at all.* You are pure light, and the depth of light is so great that it becomes *inverted* in that way. It becomes pure darkness because it is so intense, so strong, that it is just pure black to our physical eyes.

If you're a part of the Void, you have no eyes, so you don't experience that sight; you don't experience any body senses, but that is you in your primal form. As you take on a body, something happens. You take on a body, and then there is a brain that is working to portray images for you. As it's portraying images, in its most primitive state, it looks something like Illustration B. The lighter part is memory, is imagery; the *light is imagery*. Out of the pure-depth darkness of the primal being, when you take a body, then there becomes *physical* light. Without a body, there is no physical light because you are just pure light, so you're just the darkness. You take a body, and then you become this physical light.

Illustration B*
Variation: First recognition

You see this physical light everywhere. When you close your eyes, when you're at rest, you see this physical light in kind of a mottled look, like snow in darkness (Illustration B). As images come and go, this becomes distorted; it changes into various shapes; images start moving. As the stream of consciousness moves through the mind, sometimes you see it. With your eyes closed, you'll see an actual *stream* (Illustrations C & D).

*Please note: Various colors can emerge from these different types or patterns.

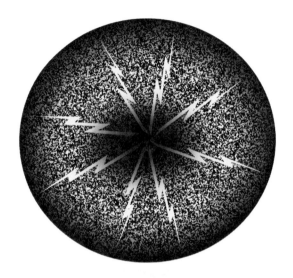

Illustration C*
Variation: Energy (light) prior to being collected

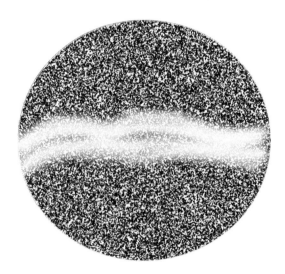

Illustration D*
Variation of Collected Energy Stream

*Please note: Various colors can emerge from these different types or patterns.

This actual stream is just imagery passing through your mind. If you're not apprehending the imagery, if you're not grabbing at it, it just 'passes through.' As it passes through, sometimes, it will take various forms; it will take all kinds of forms. You'll see things, and you'll see colors. Sometimes, maybe you'll just see this mottled look—the light and the black, but a lot of times, you'll see colors; you'll see shapes.

Ball of Light Variation
The meditator still looking in at inner dimensions

I was watching imagery last night, and I was looking at these blue streaks coming through it. Imagery passes through your mind from memory, from state of consciousness. When it's a symbolic type of imagery, like the blue streaks, that's from a state of consciousness. Memory images—(for example) a dog can run through your mind as you have your eyes closed—that's a little *light being*. It's no different than this stream that you're looking at. It's a light being running through.

You are pure light in your primal form. When you take a body, that pure light then becomes illuminated through memory images. All life is memory. If something passes through your mind—the instant that it passed through—it's memory already! You've already *had* the experience for it to pass through; otherwise, it could not pass through. You can't see anything in life that isn't memory.

You are experiencing the *movement of light*, and it's coming from memory images, even if it's symbolic. You see all these things with your eyes closed. There's really just a tiny, little bit of light coming in from the bottom of your nearly closed eyelids; they're not completely closed, but almost closed. Shut your eyes, and you'll see this mottled look...probably pretty much what I had on Illustration B, only it might have light superimposed over it. The superimposed light can be various colors, or it could be one or two colors; and all of a sudden, a little memory image will run through there. Then you say to yourself, "Oh, I have a memory image!" Don't do that. Just allow it to go through, and you'll note it. You don't have to talk to yourself about it.

Keep your attention on the light. As you keep your attention on the light, then this imagery passes through your mind. The design of the imagery is limitless. First of all, you'll see memory images—dogs, people, places, things—*based on your own experience,* which is your *karma….Your experience makes a state of consciousness,* so if there isn't a memory image in there, or the background of a memory image, it will take *symbolic form*—like a streak of blue light coming through the darkness, or shapes. It could be pyramids; it could be anything. You don't try to *make* anything happen; it just happens. That's all part of your consciousness.

Your consciousness is formed from your experience, so you begin *to observe* this flow of 'unusual' imagery; yet you've had this same imagery forever. As a kid, you probably played with it a little bit, and every time you said anything about it, you were probably told, "Oh, that's just your imagination." Your parents and your elders were unaware that this was their real *connection to divinity.* But now, you are learning to pay attention again, because this is what denotes that you're alive. If you don't see light when you close your eyes, and the light takes the form of this mottledness and a multitude of shapes, why, you're not *alive.* That's your 'proof' that you're alive.

It's also your proof that your *awareness is intact,* if you become

23

aware of it. Becoming aware of it is so multi-dimensional. *The more that you become aware of it, the more that it unfolds for you.* You'll discover all kinds of things. That discovery part is something you'll have to do yourself. Get acquainted with it.

But first, you know that what you see with your eyes closed is light, *and even the darkness is light.* Without the darkness, you couldn't recognize light. You need the contrast. You have the light coming through the darkness, and *the darkness is intense light.* You have lesser light coming through intense light. Oddly enough, the intense light comes across as blackness. Endeavor just to focus on the light; don't 'look' for anything. You'll see things, but don't 'look' for anything. Just stay open.

As you watch the energy stream, you can see if your body is erratic, or calm. When you are in a calm state, and somebody enters your space, you can see a variance in the energy stream, and that variance, by memory associations, is what makes pictures in your mind. That's what makes dreaming; *that energy stream is what makes dreaming.* We dream when we sleep; we dream when we are awake. When you are *looking out* at the world, you are in a dream, too, only the dream looks different than when you have your eyes closed. You have the energy stream, and then the fluctuations in the energy stream according to what's happening.

With your eyes open, you have energetic portrayals of objects and people, and the movement that takes place between those objects and people. It's still the same thing; *it's all light*. That's why you become *oblivious* to what's going on in your life, because you see objects and people, and you think everything is *outside* of yourself, but it's all *connected to you*. You are alive; you have this energy stream, so the very fact of what you're seeing has an effect on your body/mind consciousness. Pay attention to the energy stream that passes through your mind.

Close your eyes, and what do you see right now? You become aware of the *different energy signatures*—these light forms that exist within you—so that you can realize that the light forms that exist *within you* are what is portrayed *outward* when you open your eyes. When you open your eyes, you see a *portrayal* of the *energetic* forms in *form*. You see a form, *a formulation of energy*, with your eyes closed; but you don't see *form, per se*. You don't see objects, except as imagery passes through your mind from memory. You need to know the part that memory plays, passing the scenes through mind, but the scenes through mind shouldn't necessarily be focused upon, nor should there be a strong focus on the energy masses that come and go with your eyes closed, but you need to be aware of them. This type of awareness makes you aware of light itself. The light that you see with your eyes closed—and it doesn't matter how dark it is—if you'll wait a moment, you'll see that the light comes anyway; there's light even in darkness.

The very fact that, when your eyes are closed, you see this energy stream, proves to you that you're all light. As you come in contact with various situations, if you have your eyes open, the light and shadow appear around situations as you're interacting. The problem is you lose contact with the variance of light and shadow, because the variance of light and shadow is the same thing that you see—this energy stream—as if you had your eyes closed.

That's how it portrays in the environment. With your eyes open, you see the light and shadow, and you see movements. You see movements just like you see energy streams with your eyes closed. Only with your eyes closed, everything is broken down into pure energy; whereas, when you have your eyes open, you interpret things as people, places and objects. You need to come in contact with this energy stream inside of yourselves, to watch this energy stream. You watch the energy stream, and you will come in contact with the light in ways that you never have been in contact with it before.

How to
Meditate

The purpose of meditation is, first, to learn to sit in a repose where your body can be comfortable in some way. If you can't sit cross-legged, it's all right; but it's best if you can, because you have a certain alignment that takes place in your body that is best when sitting in that manner. But if you can't, you can sit in a chair, and in that chair, you have to find that comfortable place where your *tailbone is aligned properly with your back*, so you're not slouching. As you're sitting there, close your eyes almost all the way, *almost* all the way, and just *sit still.* Don't allow yourself to be distracted by little itches, or things of that sort. They will go away. Those are just little nerve endings pestering you. *You* are master of your body; your body should never master you.

You 'mastering your body'—what does that mean? It means that if something starts to cramp up, *you* can *relax* it. You learn to relax in such a way, without shifting this way or that way, without standing up, or without doing anything. You learn just to relax *those muscles.* When you learn to relax your body, you've achieved something very important for yourself because you've attained a *degree of self-discipline.* Self-discipline is really important, not discipline from *others.* Self-discipline means you can take charge of your *body*. You can take charge of your *brain*, so that it doesn't run off chattering away at you. You take charge of it. But in the beginning, if you can just *sit still*—whether it be in a chair or cross-legged—for a period of time that you give yourself for meditation, then you've accomplished something pretty great. That's little Step 1.

As you're sitting still, it will become easier for you to relax your muscles and to *be* still, if you have something important to do *while* you're doing that. The most important thing you can do for yourself is to *look for the light*. So you look for that energy signature with your eyes closed, only your eyes are not *quite* closed. You can still see the signature, and it will have colored lights dancing this way and that sometimes. The light itself *will dance* behind your closed eyelids, or your three-quarter- or 99%-closed eyelids. The light will dance. Watch the light. *Do nothing but watch the light!* Let the light *infuse this feeling of life* inside of you. Pay attention to the light. You'll feel really energized.

I recommend 20 minutes to *start* your sitting meditation with. Twenty minutes until you can find that light and just enjoy it. Keep your attention focused on the light. Don't become distracted. Maybe the phone will ring. OK, maybe you should have disconnected the phone before you sat down. Someone knocks at the door. Maybe you should

---

have put a note on the door, or gone off into a back room where you can't be disturbed. In other words, *you* have to take charge of *your* life. *Mastery begins with you developing the self-discipline to take charge of your life.*

Looking at the Light Stream in Meditation

Once you can find that space and time for yourself where you refuse to be disturbed for 20 minutes, you begin to *watch the light*. You see the light dance here and there. You keep your attention on the light. As soon as you start to chatter to yourself about something that you need to do, or something that you did yesterday, then you know that you're distracted. Bring yourself back and just follow the light. Get *interested* in the light. Don't talk to yourself *about* the light; just get interested in *watching* the light.

I said 20 minutes, but as you develop an attunement to the light, you'll want to sit longer, so maybe you'll go to 30 minutes in a couple of weeks, and then you'll go to 45 minutes, and then you'll go to an hour. One day, you might even sit for quite a few hours. Don't rush yourself, but do start with 20 minutes. If you have 20 minutes of successful attention on the light, when you're finished, you'll open your eyes and you'll be aware of light everywhere! You'll be aware of light and dark, the contrasts in the environment, much more keenly than you ever were before. You become aware of that, then you become aware of the energy signatures in manifested life around you. You become really aware of how these energy signatures are shifting and changing all the time.

As you become aware that the light signatures are shifting and changing all the time, you begin to look at the meaning of all this shifting and changing, and you see that all life is *impermanent.* Everything in life is impermanent. This impermanence tells you certainly about your body. You knew already that your body is impermanent, because we said you are *not* your body; you're something *greater* than that. You are *divinity.* *This* is the part of you and me that is exactly the *same. You are divinity, and I am divinity.* We're not separate. It's not 'your' divinity and 'my' divinity. It's *the* divinity. We're *all* That—*the* divinity, not a separate divinity. We're not segmented into little chunks. Our bodies give us the feeling that we're segmented: this is me, and this is you, and that's true because you have karma that makes it so. Your body is like a *composite* of all the mind stuff that you've been carrying throughout your life, and part of that mind stuff is genetics, as well.

In your meditation, if you do nothing else, just go ahead and close your eyes and watch the energy stream. When you open your eyes during meditation, know that everything that meets your eyes is also part of that energy stream, only it's manifested. Become accustomed to the fact that, when memory throws pictures through your mind and makes this little parade of pictures with your eyes closed, then suddenly the energy stream changes. Try to maintain an awareness of the energy stream. Thus, we have the key to true *mindfulness*.

If you have true mindfulness, you have an awareness of the energy stream, and you have an awareness of the images passing through your mind, so therefore, you can never get caught in *oblivion*. You cannot get into a state of fear; it is impossible. You are never looking at feelings, except as your body gives you signals, and the signals come to you from the energy stream itself. So you are using a world, now, that's not caught up in any kind of emotions or sensations, or fear of this, or angry at that, or any of that kind of thing. You have an awareness of this pure energy, and you can see that pure energy with your eyes closed, and when you open your eyes, you see the pure energy manifested. As memory interplays with that, as long as you have your awareness about you, the memories may show you fear images, but you won't relate to them, because you will be focused on the *pure* energy, rather than the *sensations* of fear itself. There's no oblivion; *oblivion makes fear*, because, in oblivion, you become lost, or at least, the world is lost from you.

When you look at that pure energy, you can see that you are nothing but a composite of pure energy, and that is why you see the energy. It is what composes your body. You're looking at the molecules that compose your body, and if you can view it as a stream, then you have order within your body. As disorder and chaos occur, it's because you are viewing it with memory images connecting to it, and as movements of other physical beings come into your presence, you can feel people, places and things trying to interact within your own energy sphere.

That is the most real part of yourselves, because that is the *divinity itself* that is holding your body together. That raw energy is what's holding your body together. If that raw energy was in a constant state of chaos, if it didn't have calmness and stream-movement going through it, but instead, just was jumble, jumble, jumble all the time, you can see how your health would be affected.

So your meditative state, and the meditative state that should continue when you are no longer in a sitting meditation, is the awareness of this energy stream and knowing that everything that is manifested around you is a part of that. It has an energy stream just as your body has an energy stream, and when two energy streams come together, there is a chemical reaction, or response. That response changes your chemical reaction, but most of the time, you're not affected by pure chemical reaction; you are affected by memory, because when you open your eyes and you see manifestations of people and things, these people and things are still manifestations of divinity, just like the pure, raw energy is a manifestation of divinity.

Learn to sit still. As you begin to view the light, it makes your mind still. That's what keeps that conversation quiet inside of yourself. Your body is still because you're viewing the light, so your mind becomes still. As your mind becomes still, there will be images that pass through your mind, but you won't be talking to yourself about them. You'll just be aware of it. Remember: the light produces images from your memory bank, anyway; but you'll see things *clearly* from your memory bank, not tainted with emotion. You'll begin to use your body differently. You'll *use* your body as a *sensory mechanism* because you'll have it in such good health that you'll walk into a place, and your body will convey messages to you about seeing, and hearing, and touching—without *any* distortions— without the mental distortions of being angry, or being lustful, or being greedy. So *you live freely!* You have a *state of freedom*, then, that blossoms inside of yourself. This is why you're alive. This is what you're alive to learn. This is why you build all these scenarios and relationships in your life. It's all about learning this: *that all matter is light; that you are divinity.*

There are so many configurations of this energy light that you contain within yourself. It's interesting to pay attention to it; because as you pay attention to it, you can develop a sensitivity to realize that as you open your eyes, you're seeing the same thing. In other words, you'll see the configuration of the energy that you had within yourself portrayed in the matter that is without (outside of) yourself, looking out of yourself. You come to realize, then, how the energy configurations that are taking place within your body produce matter.

What you might start training yourself to do, now that I have shown you different configurations on paper, you might *start keeping a little diary* of some particular configurations in situations that are of some prominence in your life—things that you're dealing with in job, and family, and other situations. As you begin to see a strong energy signature, and you recognize its prominence, and you see it on a continual basis, then you'll want to make a note, a description of what that energetic configuration looks like.

When you go outside, it's the same thing. You're out there walking, and the snow makes everything look so bright, and yet the snow gives definition to trees. When the snow is gone, the green does that, too. All of this has *life and light* to it. Everything is fanciful. When you close your eyes, the fanciful images that you saw with your eyes open will pass through, and that's delightful. You don't fixate on them, you let them pass; eventually, they will diminish. You become so absorbed in the *inner primordial light* itself that you don't need the outer fancy any more to remind you of the primordial, because the primordial is so intense.

Taking a
Primordial Light Bath

In that primordial light, it's a 'light bath.' *You're taking a light bath!* It *illuminates* your body feelings. It *purifies* your body feelings, because you're giving your body sensory rest from physical fancies, and everything becomes illuminated. *As everything becomes illuminated, your body heals itself.* You revive your health through these light baths. You'll come to realize that the deeper and deeper you go into the light bath, there's no thought, no imagery that passes through any more, and you're in this place of *light emptiness. It's light, but it's totally empty.* It has periodic effervescence to it, but you get beyond that, and *it's just open, empty, light.* You are *One with the light.* You're not separate anymore. You lose your separateness from the light, because everything is so Vast at that point.

When you return, your awareness is even sharper, because you've given your bodily sensory mechanism a rest from the senses for an hour, or two, or three, or however long you sit. You've given your body that much rest, so your outer senses are sharper. When your outer senses are sharper, that means your awareness is more encompassing. It takes in greater and greater depth and dimension. You might have had complete awareness before, but now it has different dimensions to it. Each time, the dimensions get finer and finer.

This primordial meditation, whereby you just *light bathe*, is unlimited where you go with this. If it's unlimited where you go with it, when you come back to moving about in your daily life, then your daily-life world has taken on a different meaning and a different way of expression than previously. You're always *growing*; you're always *expanding*, and you're always *so completely open*. You're completely open now, but you're completely *more* open. You're open, open, open, as everything is always becoming *more extensive*.

Don't ever be 'satisfied' with a level of meditation, because there is *no end to it*. *Give* yourself to it. I want you to *look at life as a living meditation*. You're a living meditation in a sitting position, as well, but you're shutting down the exterior and going into that interior light-bath form. So both are important. In order to truly have a greater awareness in your walking-about world, you need the practice of sitting in the primordial light. They work together. It's not so much a 'practice' after a while. It's just *sitting in the primordial light*.

A New Way of
Living Post-Meditation

Here you are—you're *looking out* at life *after* your meditation, and you're very aware of *contrasts*. Then you become very aware of what *change* means, and as these contrasts shift and change, you view the *impermanence* of life. More and more, you begin to understand that if things are impermanent, they're shifting and changing. How does that come about? As you *move* your body from one place to another, you *see different* things, and as you *see* different things, you have *seen how* things have changed. As you *do* things, things change; your actions produce change.

Consider on a deeper level that your actions produce change. The very fact that your divinity, or your spirit, or whatever you want to call it, makes you produce change in order to do things in the environment means that you're a creator. You are the creator. So, you *as a creator*, can take charge of the changes that are going on simply by being aware that there is a natural flux that takes place *constantly* in manifested form. You learned with your eyes closed that what you *saw* with your eyes closed *changed* with every idea, with every thought. With every mental image that passed through your mind, that energy signature changed; it shifted. You know that as you had change in feelings, the energy signature changed; now, with eyes open, things that you *do*, and things that you *feel as* you're doing them, produce the change in your life. You can *see* yourself now as the creator.

As you become accustomed to seeing that you're the creator, all of a sudden, the worst realization comes to you—and I mean, the worst— because you're telling yourself, "Oh, no, does that mean *I'm responsible for everything in my life?* All the bad stuff that so-and-so did to me?" Yes! It was your state of mind that brought about ill health. It's your state of mind that brought about unfortunate circumstances. It's your state of mind, and your actions, that brought about all the conditions in your life. Buddhism teaches you, quite starkly, that *all conditions are contained in the mind.* All conditions are contained in the mind, and when you open your eyes and start moving about in this changing, physical realm, as you move about and you *do* things, and you *think* things, and you *feel* things, *you are creating your world.* That means that *you* have total responsibility for your circumstances—not your mother, not your father, not your friends—but you. Your life is not the fault of the guy down there that threw a rock at you. The reason that the rock was thrown still had to come from you.

What this *living meditation* does is that, after a while, there is *no separation of the sitting meditation from the moving-about meditation.* The moving about meditation becomes an *extension* of the sitting meditation, because your awareness grows so hugely that you begin to see the variances. Things don't happen quite as fast as they did before. Before, you got involved in something, and you weren't aware of what was happening over here. You were all wrapped up in a situation, and you became obsessive about it, and you became compulsive about it, and things had to be done *this* way, and *that* way, and then you totally lost your awareness of what was going on elsewhere. But once you become aware of the energy signature, and how the energy signature is extended into the environment, you don't have this concentrated looking at something and lose awareness of other things. If you're concentrated on something, you still keep your awareness of everything else. Therefore, as the creator, you keep life as you want it to be. That's your job in being alive: *to keep life as you want it to be and to maintain health* in everything that you do. To maintain health *through* your mental awareness.

Your mental awareness, then, has deepened. You are not just being cognizant/legally sane; you've gone from 'legally sane' to something far greater. You've gone to an *overlapping* type of awareness, whereby *you are aware that you are aware.* No matter if you're concentrated on balancing your checkbook, you are still aware of other things that are going on around you. It's almost like you have 'energy tentacles' coming out of you in all directions so your awareness is taking care of many things at one time. It's going to take you a while to get to this place. It's your responsibility to take care of this body; this is *your* vessel. It will serve you only as well as you take care of it. Pure logic: you take care of your body, and it will function properly for you. When you put poisons into your body—foods that are difficult for your body to digest—it comes out of the pores in your body and makes muscles sore. Sugar will make your body more sore than anything. You can have things like natural sugars to take the place of refined sugar. When I say natural sugars, I don't mean high fructose corn syrup; I don't even mean pure cane sugar. I mean things you can use like maple syrup, or stevia. There are lots of different sugar-type substitutes, not chemicals, though. You need to keep your body so you can do things *you* want to do. People become crippled in their life because of the way they live.

Taking Responsibility
as a Creator

All conditions are contained in the mind. Accepting this is the hardest part about walking the Buddhist Path. Because it is a path that leads you to *awakening*, or en*light*enment, it means you have to take responsibility for yourself. That means you *do* make some changes as you go—probably not all in one instant. If you make them all in one instant, you're going to rebel against yourself and fall right back into the same old thing. You have to consider. You have to come to this place where you get *tired* of not being in charge of your body. If you're not in charge of your body, that means your body is in charge of you! Who wants that? *You* have to take charge of your body, and you'll have really good health your whole life. This good health, then, makes it easier for you to operate as the creator. It makes it easier for you to meditate, and *living meditation is simply an absorption of your awareness in the light.*

No matter what you're doing, you have that *absorption of your awareness in the light.* If you're playing catch with somebody, you still have your absorption in the light. If you're cooking a dinner, you still have your absorption in the light, because you're working *with* light. That's all manifested form *is!* It's a composite; it's *manifested light.* It's all light particles. *All energy particles are light particles*, so you're working with light. You become aware of the variances, and shades, and contrasts of the light you work with. If you remember that *everything you do in life is a shifting of the light*, then you'll begin to view life quite differently.

Your awareness becomes very sharp, very *awake*. That's the most important part about living meditation, because the more you use your *awareness* to view your life, the faster you *wake up*. It sounds funny, I know, to say that you're asleep, because here you are—not in your bed. But those dreams you have that just kind of happen in your sleep, that's the way life plays out, too, as a 'dreamtime,' when you think that you're awake. You're walking around, and things are just happening. If things are 'just happening,' and you weren't consciously aware of bringing it about, then you're *asleep*. You bring things about with your state of consciousness, your awareness. And if you're *not* aware of yourself bringing things about, then you're asleep. It's really logic to see that…because you are in charge of your life. No one else should ever be in charge of your life. If you give the charge of your life away to somebody else, you're saying, "Well, I'm going to go to sleep now and just let somebody else take care of me." Relationships are partnerships; they are not giving control away to each other, ever.

Without that divine signature of energy that you see inside of yourself, you're not alive. That's what keeps you alive. Isn't it wonderful to have that responsibility of taking care of yourself like that? Knowing everything that happens around you is because of your mental states, all you have to do is change *that*, make corrections.

When you sit in meditation, pay attention to the energy stream. When you have your eyes open in your post-meditation, let it be meditation, as well, by seeing everything as part of that energy stream, a manifestation of the energy stream itself. The energy stream that you have is affected by other energy streams. As people come in contact with you, and situations take place, if you had your eyes closed, you would see all kinds of movements and distortions in the energy stream that would be calm otherwise and moving in a particular direction. Of course, if you had your eyes open, you'd see movement of all kinds all around you. It's the same thing. What you see with your eyes closed and what you see with your eyes open are the same thing; it's all part of that energy stream. That shows you how you're affected by the environment, and how *you* affect the environment.

Your effect upon the environment is negative anytime that you don't have your awareness about you of the energy stream. Just because this is an energy stream that *you see* with your eyes closed, and an energy stream that *you see* with your eyes open, doesn't mean that you should be looking *at* yourself. If you are looking at yourself, then what happens is, there's a distortion. You feel self-conscious, or egotistical, but it's a self-consciousness from staring at yourself; therefore, you can't function well. Instead, you look out of yourself and you have an awareness of everything that's taking place around you that is part of the energy stream, and as new things come into the environment, the energy stream changes.

You can't quite fathom it yet, but if you develop a true awareness of this raw, raw, energy with your eyes closed, and watch how it is *all light* manifested in light and darkness, and various streams of energy, and movements of this rawness in your brain, then when you open your eyes and you see this manifestation in physical form, you realize it is the same thing. When you *truly* come into a realization of it, then you will be able to accomplish other things. Pay attention. Don't ever *not* pay attention. Don't fall into oblivion; don't be asleep. Don't get caught up in emotion. Be aware of the energy stream in its *unmanifested* form, and in its *manifested* form.

Give Yourself
to the Looking

You have an adventure ahead of you that is really powerful. If you can practice it, don't worry about 'understanding' it; that will come. You have a physical brain, so that understanding will come. It will come as a result of the practice of *looking at the raw energy with your eyes closed*. You become aware of light and how light produces—through body feelings and through memory—shapes and forms. You'll come to an understanding that you are a creator and that you create your own life.

It looks like a huge leap right now, but it *will* come to you. It *won't* come to you as long as you're 'puzzling' over it. If you're puzzling over it, you're doing mental gymnastics. All you can do is *give yourself to the looking*. You have heard me speak of the *ancient art of looking*. Now, we're into the real depth of it. The heck with taking A, B, C, D. You can go all the way to Z and *wake up*, if you just become aware of the light and observe the configurations as these body feelings change. Your body is a sensory mechanism, so these body feelings come and go as the memory interplays with it.

Don't concern yourself right now with 'understanding' anything. Just develop the practice of *looking* at this raw energy and recognizing it as light. When you truly can *recognize it as light*, then you'll start having *revelations* about it. As you start having revelations about it, your awareness, then, is developing to the degree that you're becoming a *conscious creator*. You're going to be truly astounded when you start to really *look* at it. You're going to be really astounded!

You'll notice that the light is actually *following* the motion of memory, or karma, that you carry inside of yourself! That memory, or karma, changes as your awareness becomes *full* on the pictures that you see, because a lot of those pictures are facsimiles. First of all, you'll begin to see the facsimiles for what they are, so therefore, those facsimiles—and there are a jillion of them that have been controlling you in a habitual manner—will no longer control you. *You will no longer be deluded by life!* Of course, that's what the *first stage of enlightenment* is about...*ending delusion*. From there, it goes, and goes, and goes.

Your total job here is to pay attention to the energy, and recognize the fact that the energy that you see with your eyes closed is nothing but light! That energy is *pure*. It's pure in that, if you have no internal dialogue going on, it's an exact reflection of your karma in that particular

50

instant that it is being played out; and that karma changes as you become aware of it. It cannot stay in a frozen situation; it cannot maintain the same hold over you *as you become aware of it, because that's what frees it.* You can't 'stamp out' karma, but you can become aware of the karma, or the memory; memory and karma are the same thing. You can become aware of it so that it can shift, and churn, and become something else, and move into a greater and greater, never-ending refinement.

This is all about *living meditation*, because as you see the energetic patterns—when you're developing your awareness of them—you're developing your awareness of the light. There is *no thought* involved in any of this. There is a *looking*, and that's it. If you want to call *looking* thought, it has to be thought *without words* coming back at yourself describing something. This is what you need to get clear in yourself. The minute that you start talking to yourself, you really lose the configurations and your awareness of them. You need to *work with a silent mind on this.* Don't 'worry' about having a silent mind, just simply *pay attention to the energy configurations,* and as you do, you'll become so interested in them that you won't pay attention to what you have to describe to yourself. You don't need to describe anything.

You're going to astound yourselves with *living meditation,* and you're going to be carrying it around with you as you're living life. The blind spots will go away, and when the blind spots go away, you'll know everything there is to know. Don't rush anything. Simply give yourself to *witnessing the light* in its myriad forms that take place in this raw energy. Recognize, too, that when you open your eyes, what you're looking at is another dimension of the same thing. It takes your application to bring to fruition for yourselves, however.

You can witness your own divinity by witnessing this energetic signature that takes place instant-to-instant within you. That *is* your divinity. Even if it's playing out in a so-called 'negative' way, it's still your divinity; it's just that your memory/karma bank is mutating it into forms that are higher and lower. It puts divinity in a tangible realm. That's why you have a physical body: so that you can put divinity in the tangible realm and you can *realize* that. When you come to a place of Self-Realization, you will not *intellectually* know that you are this raw energy—you will *realize* it. You'll realize it, and you'll realize that it's the same thing that exists in all living beings. It will make you *One* with everything. Deeply profound! That's the part of you that *already exists*. It's just that the *mutations* of that energy are caused by the karma/memory banks that you carry. But *through your awareness of the light itself*, and the energy that is displayed *as* that light, those pictures that have been making you

52

act out your life in a certain way, from your memory/karma, will change and flourish *as your awareness flourishes.* You don't have to *try* to do anything except just watch, and *become aware of the energy through your watching.*

Love is light. Light is love. They are inseparable. Now, you have to develop a friendship, *a relationship with the light,* until you can *merge* with it. It reveals everything. It's God. It's God/you, as well. Out of the light, comes sound, comes all your senses.

Learn…to sit in the light…until you become the light. From there, the only learning that takes place is about the nature of *self as light.*

Put aside everything else you learned. Intellectual knowledge— do you know what it is? It's knowledge of something you've *never experienced.* That's what intellectual knowledge is. Most people have intellectual knowledge of spirituality and the spiritual realms. They read it in books, but they have not experienced it. It does you no good until it is *your* experience.

*Find the light and bask in it….*Bask in it until you *realize* that the *light is you,* and that you carry that light with you…and that *all the world* *is you*, as the light. Use your meditations for that, and develop moving about life *as* a meditation for that, as well.

How the Light
is Infused*

*The Golden Spiral originates from three inward coiling
circles, actually cycles paraphrased from the culled intonation of
HÜMÜH (pronounced HÜM)* as recorded by Lao-tzu (700 B.C.E, China),
*Sakyamuni (500 B.C.E, India), Garab Dorji (55 C.E., Oddiyana),
Bodhidharma (470 C.E., China), Padmasambhava (800 C.E., Oddiyana,
India, Tibet), Longchenpa (1300 C.E., Tibet), Patrul (1700 C.E., Tibet), and
others, including Maticintin (2000 C.E., U.S.A, Canada) who compiled this
definitive text.*

The Golden Spiral is composed of light. Actually, the golden
spiral is light. At the center is its force, like the sun emitting rays of light.
The rays result from energy particles arranged in a particular way. Likewise,
energy particles can form spirals upon joining with other curved energy
particles. When curving into a spiral, the particles illuminate coiling circles,
which relate to cycles, explained later in this discourse. The cause of the
particle arrangement into three circles is the vibration produced by the
all-pervasive sound of the universe: HÜM, which intones universally as
HÜMmmmmmmmmm. This metric sound produces unending, circular,
cyclic motion. The light it brings about is golden or sun-like. The reflective,

mirror image qualities of HÜM resort to HÜMÜH.

HÜM is the original emanation from the VOID manifested as light in expression of Divine Consciousness, or that which animates sentient beings to life. The cyclic spirals that permeate space as a result of the HÜM emanation reveal the knowledge of its source or the VOID or Divinity. This knowledge has to be tapped into, but to tap into Divine Knowledge one must take command of the spiral by turning it around to redirect the light. This is not done by choosing a direction, but by turning around the energy of creation. This comes about by realizing the power of imagination and how it marks time, and then by emptying one's routine compulsion for all time. Thus, the 'turning around' is accomplished by quieting the mind.

Focus on the center is important, but focus is subtle, not rigidly fixed. This means that to focus on the VOID for Its Knowledge is important, but nothing will be gained without knowledge of the emanations.

When one manages their affairs with mindfulness, then those things that are managed through mindfulness do not overcome the light or obscure it. Without the light or emanation, nothing can be realized. It is the light emanation that illuminates the mind.

As one turns the spiral around, the efflorescence of the light increases due to the shift in angle, and the manner of turning the spiral becomes subtler because previously, one turned the spiral by controlling the inside from the outside; now one abides in the center and controls the outside.

If one can look back again and again into the source of the mind, meaning mindfulness, not attaching any person or thing to the source, then this is 'turning the spiral around' in its highest practice.

As a result of turning the spiral around, one resorts to non-clinging or detachment, which provides an overview knowledge of subtle energies. One can notice that, as they meet another being, they join, meaning the living movement of creative energy moves in and out between them. When this happens, within oneself there is an inexplicable sense of vast space, and one's entire body feels wondrously light.

After a while, the moving in and out between what has joined becomes indiscernible. If real joining has occurred, a oneness permeates, because the creative and the receptive have merged.

Observing the result from divine emergence as oneself, there comes the realization that empowerment means really seeing emptiness. When one cultivates contemplation of emptiness, the unconditional is empty; the conditional is also empty, and the center is empty as well.

Deliberate meditation, then, is the *light of consciousness*. When meditative effort is released, meditation becomes the light of essence because it is filled with light. It is then that one realizes that the mind must be emptied for the spirit to come alive, and that when the mind is empty, one is liberated from misery.

The mind is empty when one experiences that observing mind means to observe the purity of mind. Purity means untainted with unconscious, habitual energy. Then, the mind is witnessed in its original, non-dual, vital reality. Realization of this, without leaving the objects of our senses, causes transcendence to enlightenment.

Three Golden Spiraling Circles of HÜMÜH

1. The Outer Circle – *The dreamtime or mind Teachings, concerned with the development of the calm state of mind.*

2. The Inner Circle – *The space or phenomena Teachings, concerned with the development of a living, dynamic state free of distractions. This is the principal, essential focus to live a meditative existence.*

3. The Secret Circle – *The transference from ordinary consciousness to primordial consciousness.*

1. The Outer Circle matures as the initiation realization that whatever may arise or appear in one's life is merely an impression of one's own mental condition and state of existence. Apart from the organized and structured state of existence, which we identify as the environment or aspect of the world, we can obtain nothing unless our mental images are in harmony with the various orchestrations of material phenomena already in existence. It is this condition of mental harmonics that allows us to liberate and establish other variations of existing phenomena (materiality or conditions).

Moreover, everything that appears and exists always arises spontaneously, already self-perfected. Anything that is or has been added to spontaneously arising matter, is done so by mental dreaming, and is, therefore, nothing more than an elaboration or ornament on the original, primordial impression. Such ornaments are the musings from sentient life forms' karmic imprints.

This information is based on the following Teachings:

·   Karmic imprints of sentient life forms, particularly from the cognizance of human beings, are liberated or freed into existence by the karma or view of the living being that reflected them.

·   The primordial awareness inherent in the Awakened or Buddha Consciousness consists of the non-dual knowledge that exists within the immediate, intrinsic Awareness found within every individual sentient life.

·   Intrinsic Awareness is beyond all conceptions, which means that it is both uncreated and unconditional, meaning it is fostered by pure consciousness, rather than an individual intellect.

·   One discovers this unique state as being aware of self without there being subject and object, a oneself and another person, or a state that brings about duality, which makes 'self' seen as interior awareness and 'others' as exterior awareness.

·   In this state, one sees that anger is ignited by being recognized as anger, as in searching for an origin like melted butter dissolving into butter. This unique state of immediate Awareness can only be discovered within oneself.

·   Appearances may be diverse, but there is still a general view or primal Awareness, wherein viewing variations of sameness liberates differences.

The following Spiritual Practices will mature and complete the 'Outer Circle' so that one can gain entrance into the 'Inner Circle:'

(1) Give up 'notions' of right or wrong, and do not speak words to offend or to please.

(2) Shape, color, and sound make things appear differently. See through the external quality of things to realize the same underlying structure beneath all things.

(3) Maintain a spiritual stance in the face of others and conditions of involvement.

(4) Procure a spiritual place within one's heart, and stand in commitment to it.

(5) Discover the balanced state that is neither too happy nor excited.

2. The Inner Circle – In the state of immediate Awareness, we directly discover that all our visions, comprised of tiny spheres of rainbow light one sees in meditation and in life, are actually arising from within oneself. This is what makes it possible to remain in the meditative state even when a practice session is concluded, because the illumination of this non-dual state remains in awareness.

- Study of 100 secret formulas; 'secret' meaning oral Teachings.*

- This includes our vision of developing experiences, as well as our perceptions of reality.

- In such a state of intrinsic Awareness, we directly discover how we have manifested ourselves.

- When one sits quietly and becomes drowsy, they enter oblivion. Instead, when sitting quietly, look for potential. The quiet has meaning to it, but one cannot find the meaning with words.

There are three validating experiences:

1. When one sits quietly, one's spirit enters into openness, and then people are heard talking but it is as though they are far away, like echoes, yet they are clearly understood.

2. In the midst of inner quiet, the eyes blaze with light, filling one's presence with light until one's body feels invisible within it. One then knows what to do.

3. In the midst of quiet energy, the body becomes smooth like silk. If one doesn't destroy the feeling by becoming distracted, the energy will seem to soar upward, out of which will be produced an altered state.

*100 Secret Formulas available to bodhisattva students of HÜMÜH.

The following Spiritual Practices will mature and complete the 'Inner Circle' to gain entrance into the 'Secret Circle.'

(1) Through discovery of the secrets of the first practice on giving up 'notions,' one practices that there is no barrier between what is inside and what is outside; that distinctions appear superficial, through which one learns that, in collapsing differences, one can ride upon the wind.

(2) Through discovery of the secrets of appearances, one practices oneness with things and learns that, in merging with them, no harm can come from them.

(3) Develop the 'same' state of mind for all endeavors; therefore, one's aim is perfected.

(4) See only from one's commitment to experience its great heights.

(5) Explore and accept the nature of the six realms of 'beings' so that one may walk freely among them.

3. The Secret Circle – One's confidence becomes like a vast treasury, a mind treasury, filled with one's personal experiences and validations with regards to one's nature – past, present, and future, which is intrinsic Awareness.

Since light and its conditions of existence are realized, whatever one desires to know, one knows. All existence becomes integrated within one's Awareness; thus, the powers of manifestation are at hand, including the capacity to bring the physical elements under one's command. And there is concrete experience with respect to liberation, which elaborates one's confidence to become like space dissolving into space, or into the nature of ultimate Reality, like emptiness being liberated by emptiness.

*Reprint from the Introduction to the *"Secrets of the Golden Spiral"* by Wisdom Master Maticintin, Higher Consciousness Publishing, 2006.

Quotations from the Commentary on the Golden Spiral

Part 1

"While living meditation is dwelt upon in the material,...these practices, and your advancement through them, are synonymous with sitting meditation. They are interwoven into the Teachings and the cultivation of the practices....There is no difference in any of those Teachers mentioned (from Sakyamuni, 500 B.C., India, to Maticintin, 2000 A.D., U.S.A. and Canada) and what they're Teaching."

"There could be no *golden spiral* without light. It's the light that makes it possible for the spiral to appear; therefore, the light had to exist, and *out of the light was the vibration* that *formed* the spiral. *The spiral is the dharma.*"

"This is a *composite of science and spirituality*....If spirituality cannot be scientific, then it really cannot be spirituality, and if science can't merge with spirituality, then it cannot exist either. They are truly *synergistic*. The problem with science is that the minds are trying to seek something outside of spirituality, and that is impossible. The problem with people in religions is that they try to seek something outside of science, which is impossible.

That's why we are using the word 'spirituality.' True spirituality is always scientific. It may not be scientific of something that is already discovered, but the logic is herein. This is the important part: that the logic is intact....There is no such thing as 'blind belief' in spirituality. There is logic, and there is an experience with that logic, whereby the intellect is joined to bring the whole realization together."

"The...unending, circular, cyclic motion produced by the all-pervasive sound of the universe, HÜM, denotes that as *you* live life, you form *karma*. You form karma *by your actions*;...any action will produce karma....When action takes place, motion takes place; then the energy particles conform to that and then you have this *unending, cyclic motion* going on....So the only way to ever reach *para-nirvana* is not to make any action. A person sits down and they have decided that they are going to die, and they prepare themselves for that, and they go into this place where all motion stops. They do that deliberately, and then they can enter *para-nirvana*."

"The light this cyclic motion brings about is golden, or sun-like. The fact that it's golden or sun-like has to do with the atmosphere. It also has to do with *consciousness* that makes the atmosphere....*The cyclic spirals that permeate space as a result of the HÜM emanation reveal the knowledge of its source, or the VOID, or divinity.* That is something you have to intuit.

"The illustration of the golden spiral itself *appears* to be going one way, and sometimes it *appears* to be going the other way. But if you really look at it for what it is, the spiral, and you can see it in your mind, *it can be transposed in either direction,* because it is all *one direction.* Everything is really the same. Motion is set into movement by vibration; so through the vibrations that you put out, you have to redirect the spiral. Keeping in mind that the spiral has no real direction to it, but that in life it *appears* to have one direction or another…which is brought into appearance by vibration. All you have to do is shift the vibration and it appears to be going in the opposite direction."

"You know…all life is 'appearance,' because that is what life is. *All life is appearance.* It is appearance to be 'this way' and appearance to be 'that way.' But in appearance, it is all the *same;* it just *appears differently.* Just like situations *appear* differently, but there is *no* difference….Your intellect tells you there are different situations, but different appearances is what you are looking at: *different appearances.* In truth, the situations are very much the same, and they *can be shifted in energy* to have the *appearance of sameness.* That way, you know how to deal with all things."

"The appearance of sameness comes from a shift in vibrations, and that's what is being talked about here in this encoded type of language. The *shift* that takes place is merely an *appearance*, but it is a *recognition* that all appearances, while they appear to be different, are *the same*. Just like the spiral appears to go one way, but if you look at it in an *open* kind of vision, you can see that it goes both ways. Just like clockwise is not really clockwise; it is also counter-clockwise. There really isn't any direction. You can *see* that if you really know about appearances....Right there is a huge lesson in itself: to *see beyond* appearances, to *realize that appearances are shifts in energy*—that is all they are!"

"*All things are truly the same*, except that, through the shifts of energy, there are appearances of *this*...and *that*. In appearances, we become lost....What makes us lost? When we *feel* something, we become lost in appearances. We can't help that because we are alive. That's the problem with *attachment*. *It makes you see things from that attachment*. It's very painful. There is nothing worse than the pain of attachment, because it gives you an *appearance* that you *have to see*. If the attachment is gone, then you *see* that everything is really the same. It is all just appearances."

"If it looks a certain way, it is because the vibration, or the energy that is collected around it, gives it that appearance of distinctiveness. But in reality, everything is the same. Only attachment makes it seem different. Being lost in attachment is very, very subtle sometimes—a Teacher giving so much to make a student wake up. To give the student so much of themselves, the lifeblood to make a student wake up, can cause an attachment. That is a Teacher's greatest danger. The Teacher can see through it and will come out of it, but most people can't see through it and can't come out of it. They live in this world of appearances, and everything is *this* way versus *that* way, etc.,...because attachment makes those situations look different from one thing to the next."

"That attachment forms attitudes and behavior sequences that people live out. They act a certain way. They call it personality: "Well, I'm not cut out for this....The reason you're not cut out for this or that is because of your attitudes, and because of your opinions about your attitudes and the appearances you see around you. You see those certain appearances...around you because of your attachments. I want you to know how subtle attachments are. "I like to do *this* and I like to do *that*, and I *don't* like to do that." It is OK to have those things, but you have to realize that you can do *either*. You don't have to be always going *in one*

direction. You are always going in one direction because you are attached that way. You have to realize what attachments are!"

"If an attachment, or a liking, or a disliking, makes you rigid in how you see life, so that you see life as different appearances, and you can't see through it, that's an obstacle. It will appear with different appearances, but you should be able to see through it, so that those different *appearances*...cannot control you, because you are not attached to anything. You are not *attached* to likes and dislikes, and attitudes and opinions. This is the big lesson here. It is always attachment that we come back to, because it has such subtle factors. You see things *this way* so that's *the appearance* that you see normally *in everything*, and that is the most subtle of all attachments. *That's behind all the appearances that you see!* What a depth of consideration is here."

"What part of you is *not* functioning from attachment? The big question! Something that you have to probe. Probing the karma, the results of things in the 'good' and the 'bad,' is really unimportant. Probing the *attachment of your mind* to view things in a particular way is something to ferret out. *What part of you views life without attachment? What have you done today that is beyond attachment?* What karma have you made today that is beyond attachment? What viewpoint have you had today that was beyond attachment?"

"It is only with functioning *beyond attachment* that you can turn this viewpoint of the spiral to the opposite direction, that you can *adjust appearances to suit the moment* <u>*consciously*</u>. Do you function in a certain way? If you do, then you are living in attachment. There cannot be any freedom in attachment. Herein, are the appearances of the world that you see. *Whatever you see is a product of your mind*, your *mind-plays* of attachment."

"All situations can be adjusted by changing the vibration so that the spiral can be seen in the opposite direction, and it can be known that it can be shifted this way and that, and it can still be the same spiral. *This is not done by 'choosing a direction,' but by...turning around the energy of creation. This comes about by realizing the power of imagination and how it marks time, and by emptying one's routine compulsion for all time. Thus, the 'turning around' is accomplished by quieting the mind*—by letting go of attachments to how things *have* to look, or *have* to be....This is a very big piece."

"When the mind obsesses about something it sees....it is forming attachments, and it can *only see from* that formulation of attachment....That is why *openness and freedom* are important. But 'freedom' shouldn't be interpreted in a personality way: 'Well, then I need to be free to do what

I want, when I want to do it!' Doing 'what I want, when I want to do it,' *may lack complete self-discipline.* It is still a viewpoint locked in by attachment to an idea."

"*Focus on the center is important, but focus is subtle, not rigidly fixed.* In other words,...focus on your intention, but not rigidly. Nothing should ever be rigid.....You have to *live* the Teachings. That is the *only way* the knowledge comes to you."

"If you're in mindfulness, there can be no distractions. Mindfulness means that you have that *overlapping awareness* in your consciousness...*being aware that you're aware.* Therefore, your actions follow suit. Self-discipline, then, is not a problem, because *self-discipline is the honorable way to live*...noble and honorable. If you don't have self-discipline, then you are a slave to desire, which is a very dishonorable...addicted way to live."

"*It is the light emanation that illuminates the mind.* You have to follow the light; you have to follow the self-disciplined way. *To be aware of the light requires tremendous self-discipline.* Your attention is focus there. *As one turns the spiral around, the efflorescence of the light increases due to the shift in angle.* The shift in angle is *appropriate in the moment.*

That is *why* you've made the shift in turning the spiral... *because it's appropriate* in the moment. The shift in appearance is appropriate *in the moment*. You do it deliberately, and you know you have done it; therefore you are *completely responsible* for it, because it *is* appropriate, so it doesn't hurt you to be responsible for it. No harm can come, because *it is appropriate*; so taking responsibility for yourself is no longer a difficulty. It is appropriate responsibility for the moment."

"In the beginning, you try to shift everything in the environment with an analytical eye, and that analytical eye has attachments related to it. It can only function from attachment to what was analyzed, and what was the result of that analysis....But that's not necessarily an accurate perception, because it's based on your attachments, on your likes and dislikes, on the way you have personally formulated a way of seeing life. That's attachment."

"But once you *let go* of that, you start to function differently, from the *inside to the outside*. Because you have no attachments, you can see what is appropriate *for the moment*. If you have attachments, you can't see what is appropriate for the moment. If you have attachments to how things *should* be, you cannot see what's *appropriate* for the moment....What is important is what you learn, while doing something. The *freedom from attachment* that you gain while doing it."

"*If you want enlightenment*, know that it is much bigger than what you have thought it is. It means that *you can have no attachments. Enlightenment is brilliance of mind, brilliance of body.* It cannot thrive in attachment."

"*One can notice that, as they meet another being...the living movement of creative energy moves in and out between them. When this happens, there is within oneself an inexplicable sense of vast space, and one's entire body feels wondrously light.* Why? Not because you are having an experience with another person, but because you have the *awareness of the experience of sameness.* In the world, people define that as an experience of 'attraction,' the ability to 'get along' with that person. That is *not* what that is about. It is about *sameness.* We have different appearances because of the karmic situations or viewpoints that have been held. If you see *that*, then you can see the *sameness in us all.*"

"*Observing the result from divine emergence as oneself, there comes the realization that empowerment means really seeing emptiness.*

Emptiness meaning *sameness*....You can see everything as *appearances*, not so much as 'differences,' but as appearances."

"*Deliberate meditation, then, is the light of consciousness. When meditative effort is released, meditation becomes the light of essence, because it is filled with light*....When you develop the quiet mind, the attachment releases! *The mind is empty when one experiences that observing mind means to observe the purity of mind.* The 'purity of mind' means the non-clinging nature."

"When there is nothing being clung to in mind, that is the purity of mind. *Realization of this, without leaving the objects of our senses, causes transcendence to enlightenment.* It means we can still be in a world of matter; we can still be in the world of the spiral changing this way and that way. But it does <u>not</u> mean that we can be in the world *attached* to situations, and *appearances* of joy, *appearances* of happiness, *appearances* of...likes and dislikes that people have with relationships. *It is the appearances that they are attached to*—the appearances, not the people. The people are liked and disliked according to how they treat you in the moment.... 'I love you, because you're giving something <u>to me</u>,' you say. 'Oh, I hate you, because you're not giving what I want.' How fickle that is."

"But when you are *not* bound to appearances, when you can *see* appearances, but you are not bound to them, then the transcendent moment appears. Only then the appearance is not an *appearance*; it is a *realization*, and your vision becomes all-pervasive. So that is the 'Introduction' to *The Secrets of the Golden Spiral*, an enormous Teaching, which continues below."

Part 2

"Now we will be looking at the **Three Golden Spiraling Circles of HÜMÜH**:

First, we have **The Outer Circle – The dreamtime or mind Teachings, concerned with the development of the calm state of mind.** You can see how very important this first one is. That means that a lot of mental agitation doesn't have to exist."

"People have these foregone 'processes' that they like to work with in their mental states….They have a process whereby when something comes up, they work with it in *a certain way* until it's resolved. You have this *difficulty*, and then you go through this period of *mental agitation*, and then you go through the period of *wrestling* with it, and then you go through the period of *sorting things out*, and then you go through the period of *making peace* with what you sorted out, and putting things in their *proper slots*. It is called a 'process.' Many people have this kind of process. If you read a...self-help book, it may give you this process for dealing with things. The only thing is—you get stuck with the process, rather than having the calm mind to begin with."

"You have to go through this whole process, and if anything interrupts this process, then it is like you have to start over again....You don't want to keep starting over again, because every time you have to start over again, you have all of these difficulties you have to deal with all over again. Maybe they have different *appearances*; they appear to be different circumstances, but they really are the *same....You have one thing that goes on in your nature*, only one thing, and *everything else is a matter of appearances*....Every situation is always just a matter of appearances....These appearances are attachments. We have attachments to these appearances because *we see things a certain way*...and we think that is the way it is."

"If you can *see* that *things are appearances*, then you have no need to go through the 'process.' If you are aware of the appearances as you're living life, you have no need of living out a process to deal with something. That is the good news. The idea is to put aside these processes. First, recognize that you function from a process. Perhaps you even disciplined yourself at one point in your life...to whereby you would have a process and would deal with your difficulty through a process so you would not lose your mind. Now, I am saying you can go ahead and 'lose your mind,' and don't use the process. Instead, just be mentally quiet."

"If you have something come up that you need to deal with, be mentally quiet, in that, you can see the circumstances, and the circumstances play out in front of you, and you can make your directions from there. The trickiest part is when you are dealing with other people. Very often, if you have a quiet mind, you can hear the thoughts of other people; it is a 'weight,' a barrage, a mental attack....There is a crowded kind of a feeling. All the same, there is no such thing as a process to deal with it. It is a matter of dealing with the *circumstances* that are *bringing* the mental barrage, the thoughts that are coming that somebody is disturbed about. If the person with the quiet mind had not set it in motion to begin with, they would not necessarily hear it. If the person with a quiet mind set something in motion, then they hear that."

"There is another type of mental noise....You hear mental noise, whether you set something in motion or not. Everybody hears it, but not everybody *knows* they hear it. Some people thrive on it: 'Energy is crackling! It's exciting!' They love that feeling. Some people do not love that feeling. They feel it as a disturbance because they are used to quiet, at least having a quiet surrounding. They are just hearing their *own* mental noise, and they're not used to hearing the noise of others."

"So there are two ways there....One with a quiet mind, and one who has their own mental noise, but they stay away from other people's mental noise. When they come in contact with other people's mental noise, it makes their mental noise feel confused. Two different things there."

"Second, we have **The Inner Circle – The space Teachings, concerned with the development of a living, dynamic state free of distractions. This is the principal, essential focus to live a meditative existence.** This Inner Circle is a place where you put distractions aside as they arise."

"*Distractions can be desires*, attractions that take your attention *off* your spirituality. It can be all kinds of little bits and pieces of things that are disturbing you. A lot of times, that disturbance is a *rush of energy*, so it doesn't feel like a disturbance so much as it feels like a sort of *pleasure*. That type of pleasure truly is a distraction, because you get caught up in it. You can feel the energy kind of 'pulling' at you. It is pleasurable,...but it is painful at the same time, and it is a pull, pull, pull....So you find yourself being drawn to it, and because you are trying to maintain some sort of spiritual balance, you also pull away from it."

"That kind of energy you really want to keep at bay, by choice— *not by resistance—by choice*. What do you want? If you want to pass exams, you apply yourself to the material you have to learn....If you do not want what passing the exam will give you, then passing the exam or going to the school would be a distraction. But in the case of *wanting enlightenment*, anything that distracts you from being aware of your choices, and that means if you slip into an *obsessive* state, then that is a distraction. It is not what you are *doing* that is a distraction so much; it is your *feelings about* what you're doing. *It is the feeling mechanism that gets you off track.*"

"Third, we have **The Secret Circle – The transference from ordinary consciousness to primordial consciousness.**

Having touched upon all three circles, we will now explore *The Outer Circle*.

"*The Outer Circle matures as the initiation realization that whatever may arise or appear in one's life is merely an impression of one's own mental condition and state of existence*, and nothing happens outside of that. There is nothing that occurs outside of that realization. *All conditions are contained in the mind*....If you had not already set your spirituality in motion, then you would have no trek to make. You already set it in motion. We already met before....This lifetime is not our first 'get-together.'...It does not matter that you looked differently in your previous lifetime and that I looked differently in my previous lifetime. We have been together."

"We *materialize* our life, our conditions in life, by these *mental harmonics*....Your mental harmonics are what produces the vibration of those things that exist in your life. *All conditions are contained in the mind*....Each arises spontaneously, and it is a perfect replica of your mental condition. The difficulties and the good things that you deal with in your life are already a replica of mental conditions that are pre-existing."

"Everything that arises spontaneously is accomplished by this *mental dreaming.* Many times, likes and dislikes—attachments—promote the mental dreaming that you have. So if you have attachments, that mental dreaming then brings about certain circumstances and conditions in your life *from those attachments* that need to be dealt with."

"If you do not deal with what arises in the moment, then the condition turns into something else. Then you have two things to deal with. If you do not deal with *that*, then you have three or more conditions to deal with....When you insist on using a process...to solve your problems, it creates about 20 more problems for you to deal with in order to carry out the process....That's the problem with a process. *The quiet mind and direct action are the only way to eliminate the conditions you don't want.*"

"Because this is the physical realm and you are constantly dealing with other people and situations in life, you will always be dealing with arisings. The idea is to never deal with them 'as a process.' Throw the processes out. What really gets you in trouble is the process itself...things you have trained yourself to see a certain way. You deal with one appearance the way you deal with other appearances....You have the same process to deal with all these different things, and the process itself is a 'multiplication table'."

"You have to be *very direct*, but you have to be direct *spontaneously*, not as a process. *If being direct becomes a process, then it becomes loveless.* Then it just becomes hard...loveless. That's what you want to avoid: using these processes that make you 'cold' in your interactions. *Never lose the love.* The love is not a 'mushy' love; it is that *unconditional* love, but it is *conscious*. It is always conscious.....because in carrying out the direct activity of the conscious mind, you always make sure *the outcome is love* and not hardness, or coldness. That is that *unconditional love*, where you *want the best for whoever it is that you are dealing with.*"

"You never want whoever it is you're dealing with to suffer. You cannot stop someone from suffering, because they will suffer according to their own mental conditioning. But you never *want* anyone to suffer; therefore, there is no anger in you....Real love has no anger, because if there is anger, then you would want to punish. That is a huge difference there."

"Dealing with people with love, you can say anything to them, because the love is there to make it OK. If there is no true, conscious, unconditional love there, then people feel like they have been abused. So *love has to be conscious.* If love is conscious, then you can deal with all situations in life spontaneously. As you deal spontaneously with situations from that place of unconditional love, even if something does not make sense in the moment, it *will* make sense. It will always be for the good of the whole. Even though it appears, in the beginning, that it was not for the good of the whole, it *is* (ultimately) for the good of the whole, because it was spontaneously effected from *unconditional love....*Even if it appears incorrect, you will find out that it is not incorrect—if it is effected spontaneously from unconditional love—which is certainly one of the wonderful parts of *waking up.* The outcome is always for the good of the whole."

"If you are consciously filled with unconditional love, you have no selfishness...you are *self less.* You have to remove your 'self' from the dealings, and you just deal with what needs to be dealt with. You have a body that has a sensory mechanism to tell you what those things are. If you can effect from unconditional mind, then your mind is quiet to begin with. What you hear is part of your sensory mechanism that tells you what to deal with."

"The fact that sometimes what you hear is unpleasant means that you must deal with it quicker. But all things, as they become apparent to the sensory mechanism—in any strength or magnitude—should be dealt with immediately....If there is not much strength or magnitude to it, you might go ahead and let it play a little bit. Sometimes, people resolve it themselves. But if there is any strength or magnitude to it, you deal with it immediately."

"*Only if you are living from a conscious, unconditional love, can you allow yourself the trust to act spontaneously.* Because if you have anything 'for yourself' that you get out of it…a hidden agenda of something that you want for yourself, or you are doing something in an ego-driven manner…the outcome will *not* be satisfactory. It will not be for the good of the whole. That is the *simplicity* of living that Outer Circle. The *lack* of simplicity of living the Outer Circle is chaos, and using processes, and learning how to drop the processes, and suffering because you had intentions for self-gratification of some kind in your interactions. Part of the Outer Circle is the learning of that."

"Part of the Outer Circle is to learn to *see through* appearances, to see that appearances *are* appearances. *Appearances* are often driven by *viewpoints*....Seeing from *this* viewpoint, or *that* viewpoint is all *attachment*. Instead, you have to see from the *overview*, in order to graduate from the Outer Circle. You can peek and dabble into the Inner Circle, but it is mixed with lessons, then, that you still need to learn from the Outer Circle."

"*All living, sentient beings contain the seed of Buddha Consciousness.* But to contain the *seed*, does not mean that it is *awakened.* It means that the *potential* is there in all beings, and at some point, that potential will be *realized.*"

"*Pure consciousness has no conditions*....Pure consciousness is *open* and elaborated as *no limitations.*"

"We are all the same; we are all divinity. We have different karma, and the karma separates us, but our core mechanism is all the same."

"Anger is ignited by being *recognized* as anger. When someone feels sympathy for you, and you *see* that it is sympathy, you feel *weak*. If someone sees courage in you, and you see that the feeling that is being projected is one of courage, you feel *strong*. If someone perceives you as angry, you begin to feel *anger*. However, it is not just the *external* that makes the internal. There is the *internal karma* that relates to anger that makes anger. The internal karma that relates to courage makes you feel strong. The experiences that you have had are the things that dictate whether you feel strong, or weak, or afraid, or angry. If you have been abused and you feel that you need to protect yourself, you will display anger, or you will grow stoic inwardly."

"It is much easier to get along in the world if you can see similarities than to see everything as differences, or one thing as 'better' than another. If you see one thing always as better than another, then you're seeing distinctions of 'good' and 'bad,' rather than the overview. Yes, one may have a more polished quality to it, and the polished quality may be more desirable, but you can *see from the overview*, *why* that is so, and how the polished quality could be applied, *if* that was the course of action you wanted to take. All of that knowledge comes spontaneously, if you are in a state of *unconditional love*. As you quiet your mind, *the periods of quiet mind that you have, become unconditional love*, because there is no argument against it."

"*Give up 'notions' of right or wrong, and do not speak words to offend or to please.* Using language just to gain the approval of someone or to offend someone is never permissible in one who wants to live a spiritual life. Therefore, you also have to give up the *bias* of 'this is right' and 'this is wrong,' and instead, see from the overview how certain situations can be played in whatever way serves the good of the whole."

"If you can see the *same underlying structure beneath all things*, then you'll have the wisdom not to be attached to any of it."

"Do not be one person in one social circle, and another person in another social circle. Be the same. Maintain your spiritual qualities, no matter where you are or who you are with. A lot of people separate their spiritual life from their relationship life, their family life, their work life. Everything is different. It is all the same; therefore, you have the same ethics in everything you do. It makes life easier."

"*Procure a spiritual place within one's heart, and stand in commitment to it.* Come to recognize those intuitive feelings that you have, and recognize that *place of intuition* you can trust. That place that you recognize where you've had experiences and you *trust the outcome* of that, and live accordingly. Do not live against it, ever. If you know deep-down inside that something is the wrong way to go, do not go there. If there is a conflict between right and wrong, it is usually because you want to go in a direction that you know is untrue to your heart."

"That is pretty much a basic rule-of-thumb: *If you're going against yourself, there will be conflict.* Look for that conflict. Your heart is telling you otherwise. You have to see what that conflict is. You have to recognize that place in your heart. Not in your ego . It is a place where you *know intuitively* what is for the good of the whole, and as a result, how you will deal in refinement, versus gaining some momentary pleasure that is taking you in a direction that you do not want to go. Learn to know what desire is."

"If you can discover the balanced state, then you will recognize when you get too slap-happy....You will maintain some place of balance where you can pull yourself back again. There is a certain line you just never cross because, if you did, it would take you to some place that would make ugliness, or be where you did not want to go. *Know your spiritual boundaries and don't stray from that.*"

"Learn what spiritual boundaries are. You will be surprised. You might give yourself a bit more freedom than you thought. It is not the 'good' or the 'bad' rules, necessarily, that you learned from Mom and

Pop. Some of it is; and some of it isn't. So you might find you have a lot more freedom anyway, if you come to recognize that."

"Without learning to see through appearances, you can be spontaneous, but you are spontaneous from ego....So then your directness comes from ego and not from the heart, not from unconditional love. Actually, unconditional love is crown chakra, not heart chakra, but it floods the heart. A lot of times, people say, 'I *am* being spontaneous. I *am* being direct;' but that directness and spontaneity, if it comes from ego, from pride of some kind, doesn't benefit the whole. People will hate you for it. And why? Because you are putting out hate."

"When you *let go of processes*, you automatically move into *deeds of trust*. That is your training—to let go of the processes—so you can move into deeds of trust. This developing the spiritualized consciousness is simple, but it is very involved. It is involved, because you were taught so differently. Not involved, because it is difficult. It is, but that is because you were taught so differently. *That* is why it is difficult. You live differently. You were taught differently, and you practiced that other way of living *so long*. Now, you have to recognize that which you have been practicing incorrectly, learning a new way, and catching it at the same time. That is what makes it difficult."

"You don't *need* to know the answer in a moment of pressure. I often don't know the answer, but I *deal* with it. As I deal with it, the answer appears, or it unfolds in the situation, and others resolve it for themselves. I can understand not wanting to deal with it, because it is uncomfortable in the body. All sentient life tends to run from anything that is uncomfortable in the body. Human beings have the capacity of dealing with it *consciously*, whereas, lower life forms maybe do not quite have that cognizance. You have that ability to deal with it consciously, and it has to be dealt with from unconditional love; otherwise, you will have an outcome that makes dissension in the end."

"Running from a difficult situation, only makes you want to run more. People run from their problems …run and hide, run and hide…and nothing is accomplished. They don't get the relief that they wanted, because they are running and hiding. That is the reward that they get. Whereas, if you deal with something from conscious, unconditional love, then even though as soon as that is cleaned up, there will be a jillion more things happening because that is the way life is…it's OK. At least, the rewards are there—the constant fortunate karma to be able to do it even easier the next time. By giving unconditional love in that manner, people are growing and waking up *from that!*"

"That is the great benefit of unconditional love: eventually, you are able to get yourself out of having to even do it, because they will grow up *to it*....That's the deed of trust, but you don't speak of or even think of 'trusting.' You just trust. *You open yourself to the energies around.* You know you have to deal with whatever is there. Whether it be teaching, or just interacting, or communicating in some way, you just know that it will come forth. Because you can feel the premature reactions of people who are suffering through a difficulty that you have to deal with, it is normal to have hesitancy about wanting to deal with it. It is *their* energy that you are feeling. You can feel that they don't want to deal with it; they just want it to disappear. But it cannot disappear, because *they can't let go* of it. You feel it, and you think to yourself, 'I do not want to deal with this.' *You* don't want to deal with it because *they* don't want to deal with it. It is good that you know that. You have to know from the *appearance* of it *that it is not yours*....But you deal with it, because that feeling is just an *appearance* that is coming *at* you. It is not originating *from* you. It is really important to catch that. It is very subtle."

"The *scheme of life itself is quite beautiful.* It is very revealing. Every nuance reveals. This revelation that is constantly there in all appearances—it is beautiful that it exists in that manner, that the dreamtime is displayed in that manner. It is truly the *dreamtime*, because if people did not have mental imagery, none of it would exist. *All conditions are contained in the mind!* There is nothing outside of that. There is not a rock outside of it; there is not a sky outside of it. There is nothing, without that. So the scheme of it is magnificent. It is a playground for consciousness to become enlightened! That is what it is. It is beautiful!"

"The consciousness, caught in the mire of things, is anything but beautiful. It is painful. It is ugly-looking, and all these little appearances of discomfort are just awful. But the *scheme of how it operates* is beautiful. *The dreamtime itself is a gift of love.* What we *do* with it is not always *loving.*...The dreamtime, in its existence, is pure perfection. The very fact it can be played out in 'ugliness,' in the *dual* aspects, is *pure perfection*—the very fact that people have the capacity to be miserable so that they *can learn* what happiness is by going to the other direction, or from the overview. First, they go in the other direction, and then they find that does not work either, because it throws them back the other way, and then they go to the overview."

"There is a period in there, before one becomes a Teacher, where you have bliss states of living by yourself in caves and different things. You expound the Teachings in a different way—in books and things like that—and maybe in personal type of discourse. But to Teach, to get one-on-one with somebody in the trenches, that comes later. That is why you

93

---

have the impetus to go for *paranirvana*; otherwise, you'd never go for it. You'd just enjoy the bliss! *(laughter)*…All you do is exit the dreamtime."

The *Inner Circle* and the *Secret Circle* are oral Teachings, gifted by the Wisdom Master only to students who are prepared to receive them.

Secured in the Treasure Chamber,

guarded by the Transhistorical Consciousness

So signed and sealed,

by Wisdom Master Maticintin

Variation: The meditator becomes One with the Light

Other books
by *Wisdom Master Maticintin*
Now available from **Dharmavidya Publishing**:

The Heart Sutra (2008)
(Decipher the priceless wisdom of one of Buddhism's shortest and most important sutras through a fresh, poetic rendering and its profound commentary.)

Secrets of the Golden Spiral: Handbook for Enlightenment (2007)

Logics from the Third Eye: Timeless Daily Wisdom (2007)

Come Dance with Me: ***A book of inspirational HÜMÜH Buddhist stories that provide spiritual realizations*** (2007)

Shaman of Tibet: Milarepa-From Anger to Enlightenment (1986)

Awakening Stone (1982)

Life Around Us (1996)
(An illustrated book for children of all ages)

Recognizing God (1996)

Other books
from **Dharmavidya Publishing**:

Initiation: Autobiography of a Shaman-Buddhist Apprentice by Sharon Shier (2005)

To order
Call: 1-800-336-6015 or
Email:DharmavidyaPublishing@HUMUH.org

www.HUMUH.org

✔ *Check Here*

☐ I would like to receive information about other books by Wisdom Master Maticintin.
☐ I would like to receive information about becoming a student of HÜMÜH.
☐ I would like to be added to your mailing list and receive information about events with Wisdom Master Maticintin.
☐ I would like to receive *free* the Daily Wisdom Teaching by e-mail.

Please Print Clearly or Call: 1(800) 336-6015

Name: _____

Address: _____

City & State/Province: _____

Zip/Postal Code: _____ Country: _____

E-Mail: _____

- -

✔ *Check Here*

☐ I would like to receive information about other books by Wisdom Master Maticintin.
☐ I would like to receive information about about becoming a student of HÜMÜH.
☐ I would like to be added to your mailing list and receive information about events with Wisdom Master Maticintin.
☐ I would like to receive *free* the Daily Wisdom Teaching by e-mail.

Please Print Clearly or Call: 1(800) 336-6015

Name: _____

Address: _____

City & State/Province: _____

Zip/Postal Code: _____ Country: _____

E-Mail: _____

HÜMÜH™
Transcendental Buddhism
Transcendental Awareness Institute
P.O. Box 2700
Oroville, WA 98844

- -

HÜMÜH™
Transcendental Buddhism
Transcendental Awareness Institute
P.O. Box 701
Osoyoos, BC V0H 1V0